Poetic Snacks for the Conscious Munchies

Shareef Abdur-Rasheed

inner child press, ltd.

Credits

Author
Shareef Abdur-Rasheed

Foreword
Dr. hülya n. yılmaz

Editors
Dr. hülya n. yılmaz
Janet Perkins Caldwell

Cover Graphics & Design
Shakeel Abdul Rasheed
Inner Child Press

Project Manager
William S. Peters, Sr.

General Information

Poetic Snacks for the Conscious Munchies

Shareef Abdur-Rasheed

1ˢᵗ Edition: 2015

This Publishing is protected under Copyright Law as a "Collection". All rights for all submissions are retained by the individual author and or artist. No part of this publishing may be reproduced, transferred in any manner without the prior **WRITTEN CONSENT** of the "Material Owner" or its representative, Inner Child Press, ltd. Any such violation infringes upon the Creative and Intellectual Property of the Owner pursuant to International and Federal Copyright Law. Any queries pertaining to this "Collection" should be addressed to Publisher of Record.

Publisher Information
1ˢᵗ Edition: Inner Child Press:
intouch@innerchildpress.com
www.innerchildpress.com

This Collection is protected under U.S. and International Copyright Laws

Copyright © 2015: Shareef Abdur-Rasheed

ISBN-13: 978-0692555392 (Inner Child Press, Ltd.)
ISBN-10: 0692555390

$ 19.95

When you chase after the world it runs away from you. When you run from the world it chases you.

from the Prophet Muhammad, PBUH

Dedication

Bismillah hir Rahmin nir Raheem
In the Name of Allah,
the Most Gracious, the Most Merciful

This labor of love is first and foremost dedicated to the One who created me and blessed me with life, working body parts, including the faculties to think critically – that being Allah (SWT) and no other. Nothing mankind is said to be accomplishing can be achieved without His mercy and blessing. The last prophet and messenger, Muhammad (SAW) was the prototype of how we, mankind should live in this life and attain His favor in the hereafter forever.

Allah (SWT) has blessed me with a great family whom I cherish with all my heart. I dedicate this work also to them, in particular to my wife Jamillah, my life partner of close to 50 years together with whom we were blessed with 8 beautiful children. In the order of their birth, they are Rasheeda, Rukiyar, Ismail, Idris (ra), Shakeel, Ihsan, Yasin and Masha. My dedication of this collection extends to my many grandchildren (42 and counting) and my newly born first great grand daughter as well.

I further offer my dedication of this work to those who went back to Allah (SWT), Yahya (Charles, ra) my brother in-law; Naomi (ra), my dear baby sister and to Idris (ra), my cherished son. May Allah (SWT) bestow His endless mercy upon them all and grant them all Firdous; the highest level of paradise. Ameen!

Last but not least, my work here is also dedicated to the memory of my dear parents, Jack and Bella; my mentor, Dr. Anas Mustapha Al Najjar (ra) from Cairo, Egypt and my dear friend, Belal Abdul-Wahid (ra), all of whom have always stood firm on truth and justice. I further extend my dedication …

As for the poem below, its lines reveal my dedication to the precious grandson, brother, uncle, cousin, friend, and father my family and I had in my son, IDRIS MUHAMMAD (ra):

two years today
much love everyday
always in our hearts, minds, prayers
come home…

leave the world alone!

even before you were born
the plan was
that you wouldn't stay long

leave the world alone!

there are better realms to roam
roads that lead to the abode
that holds ease, peace,
bestowed on those
who remained true

Ya Allah (SWT), he lived to please only you
mercy extended from the one
who shows real mercy
but in our feeble minds,
weak hearts, blind eyes
we don't see the forest for the trees

leave the world alone!
leave the world alone!

take my hand, follow me
into a land of milk and honey!

a list of bliss that is long as
forever's going on
true peace, worry free
special trees, fruits,
treats of pleasure

streets of treasure

leave, leave, leave
the world alone!

in spite of whatever
you've been invited…

forever!

as travelers on a journey
let us all endeavor
not to live for today, but forever!

Ya Allah (SWT), forgive his and our faults
Ya Allah (SWT), have mercy on him and us all!

Aameen!

Shareef Abdur-Rasheed
aka
Zakir Flo

Acknowledgements

My humble appreciation goes to the staff of Inner Child Press, Ltd. who have been extremely generous and supportive to me and other artists.

William S. Peters Sr. ("just bill"): Thank you! You are a wonderful human being, wearing a ton of hats like publisher, writer, poet, organizer of all possible high- caliber events.

Janet Perkins Caldwell: Another one, cut from a special cloth.

Jill Delbridge, Hülya N Yılmaz; I appreciate your patience and understanding. And to the rest of the ICP staff, please forgive me if I didn't mention your name.

The whole illustrious Poetry Posse of whom I'm a member. Always a pleasure being a part of The Year of the Poet publication with all of you every month.

A special thank you to my son Shakeel on doing the cover graphics and design with William 'just bill' Peters, Sr.: Kudos to you both. My son in-law

Joe "Yusef" for always being there. Jazak Allah Khair! My daughter in-law Danielle for holding it down. Much love/blessings.

Last but not least: Thanks to all the enormously talented poets, writers, thinkers, artists of many genres now and in the past who have paved the way. May none of us let you down or drop the baton you have passed on.

Respectfully humbled,

Shareef Abdur-Rasheed, AKA Zakir Flo

Preface

What you have in your hands is not a book but rather an act of blowing riffs. This may not be what you expect. To me, my doing this in the style that I have been blessed with is a vehicle to carry a message – a message of hope in the embodiment of poetry. My poems carry reminders why we're here on earth and the best method to utilize our short but enormously critical stay here during what we call "life". In my writing, I include sentiments on social, political and moral issues but also on other aspects of humanity and what such focus implies.

Now that being said, I can get incredibly long-winded concerning the aforementioned statement but I won't. I will, instead, let the context speak for itself.

I want you to know that this effort is simply a creative expression and not a religious text. It is meant for mankind of all persuasions to digest. May Allah (SWT) forgive me, if I offend anyone.

At the end of the day this is…

food 4 thought!

Shareef Abdur Rasheed

Foreword ~ Editor's Notes

With the electronic age upon us, it is not often that an editor gets to meet the author whose draft work s/he is designated to prepare for its pre-print version. In the case of Shareef Abdur-Rasheed whose debut book, *Poetic Snacks for the Conscious Munchies* you have the pleasure to be presently holding, I had not only a delightful but also a most insightful encounter. His colorful personality and refined sense of humor had already been evident to me based on my close readings of his poetry. When Shareef, began to dance through some of his poems with his own musically trained voice and ear and experience in speed-reading, I realized he had an unintended private lesson to offer to me.

Shareef's landmark wordplay resurfaced in their consciousness-raising rhythmical persistence to seep through my stubborn seasoned-teacher-eyes. In sum: I had been refusing to comply with the author's aim all along. Until I heard him in his own environment, that is. After that critical moment, my task became obvious to me, and in the hope that it will be thus to those of you who continuously edit others – if not in writing then in your minds, I choose to share my find with you: to acquaint oneself with the unfamiliar regardless of its rule-breaking facade, before confining it to the chains of the indoctrinations of any editing mechanics.

hülya n. yılmaz, Ph.D.
Professor, Liberal Arts
The Pennsylvania State University

Links:
editorphd.hulyanyilmaz@gmail.com
www.writerandeditordryilmaz.com
www.authoroftrance.com
http://www.innerchildpress.com/hulyas-professional-writers-services.php

Table of Contents

Dedication   *v*
Acknowledgements   *ix*
Preface   *xi*
Foreword ~ Editor's Notes   *xiii*

The Poetry & The Words   1

marginalized	2
do they	4
the big picture	6
wusta	8
peace	10
gracefully	12
Five Spot	13
and	15
The Public Statement of the NYPD PBA President Against the Mayor of NYC	17
pools	18
freedom is	20
contrary	22
i implore thee	24
what's new	26
turbulence	28
justice	29
can you	31
reflect	33
what goes up ∧	35

Table of Contents... *continued*

measure	36
a lifetime	37
Amanda Madiba	39
Dispelling the Big Lie	42
in da blink	43
lost 'n' found	45
Manifestation Divided	47
many	50
it's	52
allure	54
the desensitized	56
drained of	58
like trees	60
9/11	62
separate unequal	64
self	66
you	68
living…	70
masterminds	71
floodgates	73
he vies	75
frontal lobotomy	77
i look	79
hitting the path	81
exploring	83
so…	85

Table of Contents . . . *continued*

Musafah	87
they	89
do	91
light	93
tell me	95
to rely	97
the time	99
real lights	100
lifting	101
pour	102
returning	104
a van	106
raised	107
MAKE IT TIGHT	110
in Remembrance of Sulaiman El Hadi	

epilogue 113

about the Author	115
What People Are Saying	117
The Gallery	133

Shareef Abdur Rasheed

Poetic Snacks

for the

Conscious Munchies

Shareef Abdur-Rasheed

inner child press, ltd.

When you sit next to fire you smell of smoke. When you sit near roses or musk you smell of roses or musk. Association breeds assimilation You become of those you associate with.

from the Prophet Muhammad, PBUH

The Poetry & The Words

marginalized

ostracized, trivialized, categorized,
victimized, castigated, investigated,
underrated, separated, deprived, hated

why?

rhyme nor reason does not apply
when you live in the season of the lie

those who uphold truth and justice
become outcasts among us
in a world that made the wrong, right

if they could
they would make the day, night
as it is they establish darkness
in the place of light,
giving rise to the demand to compromise

let evil rise, close your eyes
take them off the prize!

*Shaitan's plight extends the invite
to give up the good fight

to forbid wrong, enjoin right,
giving way to the light of day,
sinking into the darkest of nights
come into play
the day might make it right
and righteousness fades away

is the day a slave to your flesh
who becomes your lord
because that's what you chose to obey

food 4 thought!

~ ~ ~

Shaitan is a noun that stands for Satan or the Devil in Arabic. Various spellings occur in different Muslim countries.

do they

remember the thousands of civilians
they were killing
in Hiroshima, Nagasaki
mushroom clouds then fire storms
nuclear terror-dome
no more mommy, daddy, or a home
Palestine, Soweto, Joburg
have you heard of Rwanda?

cries when babies die
earth cooking on deep fry
life 'n' limb at a premium
no more than stepping on bugs
mass murder wiped out mother hugs
indifference intolerance replaced love
what have the people done?

you kill for freedom or just for fun,
acquire wealth 'n' power
at the point of a gun?

are stars 'n' stripes the logo
for tanks and guns?

with the people's blessings
the carnage goes on
as it's business as usual back on the farm
"get ya hotdogs 'n' genocide here"
hotdogs and genocide here
wash it all down with napalm beer!

why the f[…]k should you and i care
a few thousand slaughtered here and there
all for freedom, right?

hey you told us that's why we fight
raise your beer and give a cheer
it's Memorial Day and Blackwater!

Halliburtons here
hip hip hooray
might makes right win the day

food 4 thought!

the big picture

is Allah (SWT) in full control
regardless of what it seems
as far as there are extreme
times and human beings
doing things that defy reason
there's always a plan
organized in full effect
a fact we may not fully overstand
but got to respect

what did you expect
paradise in the present tense?

instead,
this is the time of a test, a trial
a time extremely stressed and vile
istiqamat* is the one and only style
knowing no matter how it seems
Allah (SWT) is in full control
all the while
adversity redefines, refines, redesigns,
underline what kind of iman**
truly is yours and mine
while ease and comfort stagnate
our spiritual status
times of test teach us all about us
in a time Islam is defined
as the scourge emerged to scorch the earth
"Muslims have been mad from birth"…

it's extreme to obey the word
to apply literally equals insanity
such is the promoted accepted mentality
to self indulge restriction-free is normality
believing we're in full control of our destiny

how blind it is to define the word divine
outdated, out of line, a blip in the script from another time

come let us indulge, wine 'n' dine
never mind the time, we will die!
let's not think ahead to tomorrow
the day of regret and sorrow!

no one can undo
there will be no more time
to steal or to borrow
this is the real deal that awaits
a people void of faith
that thought they could avoid their fate

food 4 thought!

~ ~ ~

*istiqamat: The word that defines the state of being steadfast in Arabic.

**iman: The Arabic term for "faith".

wusta*

signifies balance,
patience deliberation
hikmah** liberates one
from what haste makes
waste made from mistakes

take the case at all costs!

impatience brought results,
leaving humans distraught

on second thought…

was a lesson taught?

balance, not to be ignored
as has been the case…

though constantly implored,
mankind remains lost,
charting the same course of the insane,
elects to remain in haste
then wonders why the pain
that came from waste
over 'n' over again

makes the same mistake
on the real deal
even though that's real pain
he/she feels
fails miserably from the inability to see,
rendered blind

hikmah is not taught
in any university you'll find
it's a gift bestowed from the divine
upon those Allah (SWT) chose
and he only knows why

balance, moderation, patience,
avoiding the suggestions,
intimidation from Shaitan's invitation
always made fair
seeming pleasing to the eyes
in an attempt to hide the real reason
in the darkness lurking behind,
trying to be out of sight, out of mind

food 4 thought!

~ ~ ~

wusta: A Kuranic term assumed to translate into the English as "middle", as in a balance.
**hikmah: A noun meaning "wisdom" in Arabic.*

peace

broken, smashed, violated,
ravaged like a virgin,
taken by blunt force
such is the train wreck called
man has done everything
to define brutality
frequently
to the extent to attempt to reinvent normality
plotting new skewed, altered views of sanity
using what they can as a tool to fool 'n' demean
to fulfill their evil dreams
to amass vast wealth and power
to maximize their means
way beyond their needs
always looking where they can plant
evil seeds to grow into lethal apparatus
to impede peace
right under the nose of people
without them knowing a thing about it
because to those who possess this disease
peace is something they don't want nor need
because peace creates a climate
that exposes ravenous motives
that thrive on lies that prefer to hide
on the dark side
turmoil and fitnah* create diversion
while greedy enterprises have means

to put up a smokescreen
while they rob the needy clean
to further enhance their already fancy gains

things ain't never what they seem!

food 4 thought!

~ ~ ~

fitnah: A noun in Arabic generically translated as "mischief".

gracefully

bow as the curtains come down
on the reality of mortality!
for it is meant to be for certain
certainly, curtains come down permanently

then the encore goes on forever,
depending on the pleasure of
the Supreme Critic's critique
lies the fate of the so called late

however the performance rates,
mercy may be bestowed,
giving a glowing review
on behalf of you

it was written the world's a stage
all have a part to play
you fumbled your lines in your presentation
you played around and neglected the essential preparation
or you spent the time wisely,
studying lines to deliver a sublime performance,
making the best of your time
before the curtains came down

lights out
you left it all on that stage
the part you played

the question remains
what good from it can you take to the grave
or was your performance a total waste?

food 4 thought!

Five Spot

it was '63 me and Pee Wee
got on the tubes, Journal Sq.
seeking tunes everywhere
not Funk 'n' Pop
but Monk 'n' Bop at the Five Spot
St. Marks ain't a saint it's a place,
a place where Be-Bop was in the air

so me and Pee Wee got on the tubes
could hear the tunes
in our head long before we got there
set 'em up tables 'an' chairs
it was your room only with a spot
cleared out for the bringers of groove,
cool, "riffa'lutions" of 'round midnight,
Stella by Starlite, Monk's Dream,
Green Dolphin Street
Thelonious, Mingus, Hubard, Roland
blowin' 3 horns, Sunny, Max, Elvin
Jones, you was in your crib chillin'
with hard bop masters intimately,
performing lyrical miracles
the Five Spot, me and Pee Wee,
Eric Dolphy, Charlie Rouse, Trane

dam dat was dope!

Poetic Snacks for the Conscious Munchies

1963, East Village, near the Bowery
the place on St. Marks Pl is etched
in 3/5th's time
like a crepicle with Nellie in the epistrophy
stolen moments in melodic history
in the archives of my mind

never will there ever be that groove again!

food 4 thought!

and

the people suffered through another day
same ol' same ol' what can you say?
that's the game the bastards play
this is the MO the devil's way
in the good ol' U S of A
sooo it's the same ol' sameo
you and i know sooo well
many live a living hell

how many you know ain't doing so well?

but to listen to the story the spokesfolk of glory tell
the impression in spite of blatant oppression is
"Oh Well"
"this is a democracy", they say,
everybody gets a play
in the good ol' U S of A

it's your call today
depending on how good you play "The Game"
regardless of your color,
social economic status, or name…
"All for one, one for all in the good ol' U S of A"

so they say

but if you live in it from day to day
in the 'hoods shrouded in dark clouds
that speak a different tongue
know all too well
the yoke that's hung

around the neck of old 'n' young
who rarely get respect
try to make it through with the government's check
in a 'hood with no resources for you
no libraries, parks, rec centers, or schools,
if they used to…

now stay boarded up or closed after dark
no mo money in the budget, they say
but ain't a war, prison, or police equipment
they wouldn't pay for

and the election time rolls around again
and everybody's "your friend"
and "You vote for me, I promise we'll spend
to get what ever you need!"
"You hear me?"

don't ya'll worry
it's gonna be okay
after election day
in the good ol' U S of A!

food 4 thought!

The Public Statement of the NYPD PBA President Against the Mayor of NYC

NYPD, especially the PBA has exhibited how deeply rooted and systemic racism is entrenched in not only the NYPD but in American society in general. It's a psychosis, an advanced chronic condition. When the mayor expressed that Eric Garner or Mike Brown for that matter could easily have been his own son, the president of the PBA said that statement constituted the same outcome as "throwing the NYPD under the bus". The condemning of the mayor followed with a statement that he was not welcome to attend any cops' funeral – which has been a long standing duty of any mayor of NYC previously. This reaction shows how deeply sick the Para-military organization is, probably the largest PD in the world. That response by the leader of the PBA reflected on the attitude that the NYPD has carte blanche to kill and maim at will, especially in the Black and Latino communities without ever being held accountable. For to this day, such act stands as SOP: "Standard Operating Procedure".

pools

of deep red life spilled at will
blood running wild by beasts
unleashed to kill, maim
inflict pain
on women, men and child

look at the bodies pile
get higher than the tallest mountain
in a while
if that hasn't already been compiled

meanwhile back on the local
it's real but surreal,
priorities twisted
as the sheep are herded
into the world of plastic
seemingly oblivious to
worldwide carnage, pervasive
rather than deal in the unreal world of the evasive
calling it free, but actually be slaves
to their craves

will come back
to bite dem in da grave
try to tell dem to behave
appreciate gifts Allah (SWT) gave
the beautiful life he made
the earth's bountiful
blessings uncountable
more than enough for all on the real

but greedy man's evil
doesn't ever deal fairly,
led by Shaitan
has driven mother earth into despair

mankind the same that came from a single pair
mankind the signs are defined so beware
to obey do what the wahi* say
when you hear and see signs appear crystal clear
realize time flies by
and there is a purpose
why we're here!

food 4 thought!

~ ~ ~

wahi: "revelation" in Arabic.

freedom is

submission, suppression, abstention
submit to Allah (SWT) commandments
suppress carnal desires
abstain from forbidden things

freedom is obedience, compliance

freedom is not to be free
to be a fool
letting your desire rule
being in a constant duel
with what you're supposed to do

freedom is a fight with evil
not about how we feel

the price of freedom is real
real is called "struggle"
but it can only come from
the one and only one
only he who gives you life
can set you free
not the rantings of empty
so called patriotic slogans of any
nation or country
only the one who gave you life
can set you free

you have to give up
that which you love to attain Al-Birr*
it's called "sacrifice"
righteousness=freedom

freedom ain't never free
only the one who gave you life
can set you free

food 4 thought!

~ ~ ~

Al-Birr: righteousness in Arabic.

contrary

to popular belief,
the words of the wahi
apply to all situations today
and in no way are played out,
antiquated or outdated permanently
but instead
remain contemporary
and sustain potency

truth remains truth
falsehood is falsehood for eternity
a sign of it's legitimacy and longevity

a rhyme in recognition of the wahi
withstood the test of time
but mankind has ignored that
which was sent to guide and warn
in fact reacts with scorn
making rejection of it the norm
instead, prefer to conform
to what men invoke
falsehood, misguided words spoke

pulling many away
is the promise given
when Shaitan broke his contract
with the only one worthy of worship,
promising turmoil and mischief
until the day of reckoning
it will insist on a shift
that flips the script

read the words of the Qur'an
bite down on it!
hold on tightly to the rope of Allah (SWT)
to the words that Allah (SWT) spoke!

legislation invoked with the stroke of His pen
and then the pen was put away
the ink dried

everything revealed apply until the Judgment Day

can't add or take away
to what Allah (SWT) did say
words of Allah (SWT), heaven sent
are and will ever be relevant

food 4 thought!

i implore thee

endure!
for a little while more
life has much in store

you'll see
after difficulty
comes ease
twice as much

change hovers above
as we engage in love of ease,
of self indulgence
that which creatures of comfort seek
as we speak

paradise here on earth
blot out the finite fitrah*,
attrition
a given from conception through birth
then death appears to grab attention
until then reality has no place
in the daily pace

prefer to erase
refer to euphoria
fleshly sensation
immersed in the deception
of instant gratification

life rehearses the oft repeated verse
you forgot what came
with the same package received at birth

death looms

always the thousand pound gorilla in the room
to remind the conscious few
what awaits on the other side

the real you
left pleading
not the illusion we create
that dissipates
fleeting

food 4 thought!

~ ~ ~

fitrah*: An Arabic word with no exact English translation but is widely accepted as expressing the elemental human nature.

what's new

and becomes old before the day unfolds?
is it real what we hold
or is it
void of substance like foam?

habits taken from pagans of old,
carried over, respected
without origin, inspected,
no thought process reflected,
lock step accepted

the outcome of the following creation
is misguided nations
who blindly embrace the way of the ancients
the work of Shaitan's secret agents
who go about the earth and plant
falsehoods and deceptions

camouflaged as good, being accepted
made attractive, gleaming
such is what Shaitan is scheming
to make that which is evil fair-seeming

so the sheeple take blindly
what they're receiving
misguidance, the result of disbelieving
in an age where truth fades away
they listen to what fools say
the more they lie, the more they get paid

a solitary voice that speaks the truth is cast away
all is prophecy fulfilled today
awaits the fate
that's Judgment Day!

a culture born of lies
embroiled in deception
prone to fantasize
eventually must fade away
and die

in the end only the truth survives

food 4 thought!

turbulence

permeates perpetually, purposely,
is planned, premeditated, predisposed
it's supposed to flow
let ya know that's life's MO

turbulence rocks,
socks complacency
wakes up da lazy
forces pro-activity
that's the upside of difficulty
based on the fitrah of humanity

like it or not it's what you need
because human beings adore living
comfortably

turbulence
awakes
shakes 'n' bakes
lets you know struggle keeps you humble
feet firmly planted on the ground
on the journey always,
bumps on the ground
danger abounds
travelers are here to travel
not to hang around

food 4 thought!

justice

in amongst the lost rights
somewhere up in the heights
where there's divine presence,
a glorious light,
where darkness does not exist
all inhabitants co-exist in peace,
free of all human spiritual, mental,
physical disease,
evil in all forms, forever gone
the norm: never a sunset,
always sunrise, bright
after the new dawn's light

each and everyday you're reborn
nowhere is the scorned, the forlorn
everywhere bliss is getting it on
everything's right, never wrong
dark nights?
what for?
don't need 'em anymore
eternal light, highlighted by eternal life

and so you thought this life is it
if it is what's the reason to live
if life inevitably ends quick

no matter what age was achieved

compared to infinity?

please!

what would the purpose be?

birth to death
life in it's totality

so temporary hence
does it make any sense
all that without a consequence
would be a lifetime lived
without any relevance

food 4 thought!

can you

expect anything from human beings
who are hot one minute
then the next colder than a deep freeze?

what do you expect from weaklings?
did you really count on feelings,
clean hearts comprised of spiritual parts?

godly virtues would facilitate that
but how often do you make contact
you'd be more likely to find treasure
on the sea bottom
before you find virtue in Sodom

the time is coming near
where sincerity in the earth will disappear
alone with godly fear

knowledge of substance will dry up
it won't hardly be around
as the human race goes
into a deep dumb down
liars and thieves will be believed
the righteous, treated as disease

modesty, ceasing to be,
immorality, a reality

as the earth races towards calamity
clones in lockstep, blind
leading the blind over the cliff
ears, eyes and minds, rendered useless
because the deaf, the dumb and the blind don't use it

that time is not drawing near
that time is here!

food 4 thought!

reflect

on the sound
beauty resounds
blessings all around
listen to them fly
in the sky

lovely voices sing out
as they go by or perch
serenade with sweet refrain
over 'n' over again

hover above
expressing love
giving praise
to the one above
He who brought it in the first,
the beginning!

when nothing had a voice
nowhere, no ears to hear
then brought it all here
from nowhere
said "be" and it appeared
trees, sky, creatures of the sea,
creatures that fly, crawl on the ground
beauty all around

Poetic Snacks for the Conscious Munchies

look, listen
sound resounds
blessings abound
bounties astound
beauty resounds!

food 4 thought!

what goes up /\

comes down \/

sooo

be fundamentally sound
keep your feet firmly planted
on the ground!
you're not a kite in flight…

sooo

don't try to float around!
like balloons
they look like they'll climb to the moon
but fizzling out in no time is their doom
can't depend on them to last
like many things that come and pass
in bunches, available in abundance
but always void in substance
like foams on the ocean
soon to dissipate in the water's motion

don't float like a balloon,
making moves on a notion
that ultimately ends in ruin
as often does
when we live by compulsion

food 4 thought!

measure

time relative to the days of our life
where do we stand in the vastness
what semblance of relevance
how can we claim importance
how vain, our demeanor
substance evades us
manifests in our behavior
trivial pursuit, our endeavor
for which we labor
oblivious to that which is major
obvious, the manifestation of ignorance
displayed deeming godliness,
goodness irrelevant
by what we do more than what we say
got lost in the sauce
trampled in the fray
too blind to discern the difference
between night and the light of day
deliver us from evil, we pray
mere lip service i fear,
if crops, harvested from good seeds,
planted by righteous deeds
never surface
such is the difference between substance
and that which is worthless

food 4 thought!

a lifetime

flashes by, bam!

but moments
can last a lifetime

things happen fast
can't take a thing to the bank
that's in this life,
except death

better yet never say
you gonna do so & so,
go somewhere or whatever, wherever
be with whomever
love, hate so 'n' so forever,
say nothing without insha' Allah*,
by the will of The One!
Allows us what He will.

what's around the corner,
waiting for ya?

we get caught up in the elation of feelings,
emotion misleads us with what it feeds us
fulfills the need with a short burst to tease us

that
we misread!

what's around da corner
waiting for ya?

can't take a thing to the bank
unless you get mercy
that nobody deserves

see

ya'll best be cool and grateful
and give thanks!
always reflect, get still and chill,
relax, surrender,
let your maker's will take over
and control ya!

what's around da corner,
waiting for ya?

food 4 thought!

Amanda Madiba*

some are called for a certain test
blessed with what stands out from the rest
touched, blessed.
tasks heaped on
that few men think on,
speak on,
much less act upon

Madiba, Madiba Rolihlahla Mandela
Rolihlahla, Xhosa – for "Troublemaker"
Xhosa, a son born from the royal line,
a chosen one,
leadtakers' time!

Amanda! Amanda! Amanda!
Freedom! Freedom! Freedom!
was the cry

let my people go!
we won't take it no more
apartheid must die
even if we as well
better then existing in this hell!

to try and die is worth the try
think of the story they will tell

Madiba was the one
upon whom the task fell

and soon was heard
the freedom bell

Amanda! Amanda! Amanda!

amazing cry
burning in the belly of the beast
raised to a boil, heard 'round the world
north, south, west, east

Amanda! Amanda! Amanda!

amazing cry,
as worlds leaders knew and stood by
watched many, many die
as we learn,
more concerned about the gold they buy
willing to be in bed with living a lie
was nothing new
this is what they do
what their used to

Soweto, the mines, Joburg

have you heard
young lions wanted to live but prepared for dying,
rather then exist?
to make apartheid cease and desist
was worth trying

overcome fear!

and Madiba, Rolihlahla was put away for 27 years…

Shareef Abdur - Rasheed

until the day was to be when he walked free
into the arms of Winnie and a sea of humanity

quite a journey for a man
who was picked to pick up the relay stick
and run,
carry a nation into the sun
almost 95 years from the day he appeared
and yet even today
no matter what they say

apartheid is still not done

reflect on the ripple effect,
the work of Rolihlahla,
the "Troublemaker"
has just begun

says da beat of the African Drum

Amanda! Amanda! Amanda!

food 4 thought!

~ ~ ~

This poem is dedicated to Nelson Mandela, the Winnies and Steven Bikos and the many whose names we don't know.

Dispelling the Big Lie

There is one race – human. You can't have races within a race. Allah (SWT) calls us "Tribes and Nations" as stated in the Qur'an, 49, 13:

Oh mankind, I made you into many tribes and nations that you may know one another (not despise one another). The best of you are the ones who are most devoted (Taqwa) to me.

Allah calls all the tribes and nations "Mankind", all from Adam (Aws) and Howa (Aws), as written in the Qur'an: 4, 1:

This is what we (Mankind) is comprised of, nothing else! The kufr devised this concept (races) as a tool from Shaitan to divide humans and cause suspicion, Kiba (arrogance, pride) in "my race" as opposed to "your race". This connotation automatically divides human beings, causing one group to eye the other as "alien, the other, etc", always with suspicion in a condescending way. It was devised to do exactly that in the conscience and sub-conscious.

The world over makes up the "United Snakes", comprised of "Nation States" who all buy into the big lie. Curtis Mayfield called them "educated fools from uneducated schools".

Unfortunately, Mankind (Muslims and non Muslims alike) have bought into this lie that appeals to the humans' lowly desires, the human weakness and tendencies, etc. that Shaitan exploits and preys on.

in da blink

flip da switch
switch da flip
here today
nowhere tomorrow
live da dream
today, tomorrow
nightmare, sorrow

you know,
what's around da corner,
waitin' fur ya?
and here you are
feelin' smug & fit
talkin' mucho s[..]t
somebody asks you
you say, life's great
i'm livin' da dream
know what i mean?
couldn't be better!

couldn't be better?

you actually believe
your s[..]t will last forever?

what ever!

name it!

41K, timeshares,
get-aways, silk underwear,
cribs, rides, ass,
wine, dine, etc!
none of that $[..]t lasts,

Poetic Snacks for the Conscious Munchies

past the last breath

death is da switch that flips
everybody's script

you need more than material acquisition
to make the impending, inevitable transition

smooth!

so it behooves you to be wise,
think smart

so that
your beginning
may start
with a happy ending

truth be told,
money, silver, gold
and all things considered,
are nice
but can't acquire that
what's valued
don't have a price
to be sold and bought

think at least twice!

this is…

food 4 thought!

lost 'n' found

clowns in tux 'n' gowns
get around town,
play around and fiddle while Rome burns down,
thinking if they play loud
they'll drown out the sound
of the empire crumbling down

meanwhile folks look around
for what crumbs they can find
so they don't die,
and you ask why you 'n' i
can't solve this riddle?

what you don't know will kill ya!
the same ol' same ol'
otherwise known as the status quo
disguised
so to monopolize
the cash flow
right out from under your 'n' my eyes,
out of sight, out of mind,
too blind to use your mind,
just trying to survive
while they continue to kick our behind

it's da same ol' same ol' song
while Rodney asked, "Can't we all get along?"
Marvin asked, "What's going on?"

Poetic Snacks for the Conscious Munchies

on an on 'til the break of dawn,
and you don't stop, till the top's on the bottom,
and the bottom's on top

food 4 thought!

Manifestation Divided

In AmeriKKKa, you are constantly being reminded of the reality of racism, depending on in which America you live in: America or AmeriKKKA. "America, the beautiful, this land is your land, this land is my land" depends on which of these two Americas you are in. That is because this is indeed a divided land, a tale of two countries. One is the country of the "White Privileged" for the so called White Americans; the other, for people of color, in particular from African descent. Racism is as AmeriKKKan as apple pie and baseball, and yes, it's alive and well today, now. Having black faces in high places including the Presidency of the United Snakes don't change that fact.

The Manifestation of this is the reality of two different experiences. The so called white folk who have children never have to even think about things that Black Americans know all too well. Like telling your young teenage or even younger children, especially male children what to do if confronted by the police. How to behave so they won't get shot and killed on the spot if they are lucky on a good day. The reality of driving while black or even walking while black. The profiled "Stop & Frisk" was made famous in New York City but actually is practiced all over the country. It's called racial profiling for a reason. Look at the numbers who are victims of this and you see the glaring disparity. The amount of people of color who overwhelmingly are the target of this racist policy who actually are found in any way to have probable cause to justify their stoppage, detention, etc is miniscule at best. To add salt on this wound is another insane fact. A simple stop can be fatal. In this case, being a person of color, especially a Black American becomes "probable cause".

All the while this is going on a couple of miles or even blocks away on the proverbial "other side of the tracks", the so called white folk live in an alternative universe, oblivious to all the above aforementioned realities. Whereas the police use the approach to police work called "serve and protect" in their neighborhoods. Not so in communities of color, especially in the urban areas of this nation. In these communities, the approach approaches that of a military invasion via occupying forces.

The simple fact is the average cop in this country who has such a sensitive job as policing doesn't identify with communities of color. Their mama, poppa, uncle, aunt, brother, sister, cousin, etc don't look like "Dem People". Consequently, they don't see black folk and other people of color as human beings. They will deny this fact until the cows come home but the proof is more than in the pudding.

Just like in war-torn areas of the earth like Syria where they will answer in the affirmative, when you ask any person, if they have friends and relatives affected by the raging ongoing conflict. That is the same situation in communities of color and especially young black men in the good ol' USA when it comes to them personally, relatives, friends who have been harassed, beaten, arrested, profiled, targeted. In that case, you will be hard pressed to find an exception. My own family included in being targeted by racist gangs and the police, was beaten, arrested when they were attacked, making them the criminal instead of the attackers. Facing time, they were offered a deal in the famous hallway where most cases are determined and in the case of most young black and brown men and women in this country even more so. We went to court for years, refused any deal, went to trial, cops exposed as liars, get acquittal as a result by an all white jury. Very rare indeed in the case of young men and women of color. We were blessed with the Creator's help and those supporters back then in the late 80's to 1993 who came out, including Rev. Sharpton, Alton Maddox, Lenora Fulani, Yusef Hawkins (killed by a racist in BKLYN, NY), father Moses, the F.O.I of the Nation of Islam, Sunni Muslim brothers and sisters, etc. Most folk are not so fortunate.

many

come and go in this life
it's all in the flow of this life
as the clock ticks time drips
like hot butter off a knife

you ever think about that?

no not what's in your wallet
what do you have left in the bank of life?

that's all
is your next breath your last withdrawal?
in an account
you don't know a thing about
one that you can't put a thing in
to replace what you took out

time is what i'm talking about

but righteous deeds are the seeds you can plant
it's the currency you need
when the next life succeeds this one
that quickly passes into the past
the things you covet now
will have no value
the material things you value now
won't mean a thing tomorrow
all that you cling to will ring hollow
invest in that which after death
brings you life again

you won't find it on the market
or in any land
and precious gems, limos with bars in them,
cocktails with influential friends
all that will prove worthless in the end

you ain't got no time to waste time
present status does not matter
when in a heartbeat
it'll be all gone in the former
and can harm you in the latter.

food 4 thought!

it's

good trying to grab just out of reach
should make effort
temporary failures teach
with patient eyes to see
inconsistencies of reality

what's now may or may not be the same
if today's ecstatic,
tomorrow's pain
today sun, tomorrow rain
never refrain from trying
again 'n' again!

reaching beyond
ignoring what's hard
even your body and mind feels
like falling apart
knowing that's just the start
not to be faint of heart

show faith, courage even then
when it doesn't appear smart
in the minds of weak @ heart

won't roam out the comfort zone
too scared to leave the b!+(#!Ning alone

but if they won't reach
they won't grow
if they dare not go
where others won't go
the true meaning of life
they will never really know

food 4 thought!

allure

calls all, tactics drawn
to what attracts you
so you react to
without thought of tomorrow
smitten by lust that blinds you
invited to leave all good behind you
as if falsehood becomes truth
just to satisfy you

but when the truth hits ya
what you gonna do
when reality makes a move?

does lust possess substance
to remain sustainable?
can it facilitate the peace
that needs to be attainable?
or just like foam on the sea
disappears when you hold it in your hand?

lust is the mirage in the desert
that turns water into sand
never really real to trust in
to allow lust in
to invite you to stray away

is it worth the price you pay
on the Judgment Day
when all your deeds, on display,
are put on the scale to be weighed?

consider the price that's paid
the next time lust makes a move
inviting you to stray away from truth

food 4 thought!

the desensitized

lack sensitivity
to all ills of humanity

as though
what you can't see
won't hurt me

better it's you than me!

like being…

deprived of human dignity
not to mention going hungry

life, pursuit of happiness, liberty

snatched!

by tyrannical rats
who rape, plunder,
murder without intervention,
or prevention from anybody!

with the means too

just to name a few:

Rwanda, Syria, Darfur,
South Africa, Palestine,
Yugoslavia come to mind

makes you wonder:
why?

the reason, motive behind

the so called civilizations' blinded eyes

you can bet your bottom $ollar

there's a prize in there somewhere
for dem to collar!

life and limb mean
nothing to dem
who don't care what they do to
acquire, pile up, control
wealth and power

vast!

even if it costs every precious life

right down to the last…

food 4 thought!

drained of

feelings, emotion, meaning,
what does life mean to creatures
who resemble humans
but behave like drugged demons?

void of love or respect for life
live by the gun and knife

murder, rape, plunder,
destruction without justification
lusting, feigning, not in touch with human feelings,
numb of sensation

makes you wonder…

they call them armies
they call them soldiers
some even call dem warriors

but these are labels of respect
badges of honor

how do you bestow that on
marauding armies who murder
innocent babies and women
they call mommy?

out of sight out of mind!
genocide is on the rise!

Shareef Abdur - Rasheed

out of sight out of mind!
genocide is on the rise!

while we play our lives away
on our behinds we lay
humans being slaughtered everyday

don't be surprised in time
it's you and me someday
but by that time there may be
no one left to say
so much as a rhyme,
so much as a rhyme

food 4 thought!

like trees

growing tall in the forest
created by the supreme artist

are the young, growing tall
children, grandchildren,
on the set by Allah's (SWT) willing
dem to be like the fruits
picked off da tree
that supplies nourishment

their presence supplies encouragement
life, energy, exuberance that infuse into your heart
like a life, jumpstarted, recharging,
pumping love

family is a gift from above
it's all love,
one for all and love flows

like water that helps crops grow
popping up like rising dough
have you been looking up, like, yo,
where did the time go?

only Allah (SWT) knows!

enjoy love, help one another now
while we're still around
from second to second
you just never know
what's going down
who knows
here today gone tomorrow
used up all the time
you and i could borrow

don't cast yourself into a state of sorrow
because
instead of doing what you could today,
you delayed and waited for tomorrow

and too late…

tomorrow never came!

food 4 thought!

9/11
A Reggae Blow

must keep dem busy
flood dem brains
remove peace from equation!
reap whirlwind on nation
behooves you
steep dem in inflation
make life irritation
dem live frustration
numb dem! see?
'til dem have no sensation
dumb dem! see?
give dem brain mutilation
dope dem!

no hope then…

pretend you befriend dem
intend to upend dem!

dem people
evil Babylonians offend dem

9/11 dem,
9/11 dem!

MURDER! MURDER!

seeee?

CONSPIRACY!

IGNITE THE FIRE!

MURDER!

9/11 dem!

dime a dozen dem
don't find, don't recognize
put a buzz on dem
easy to find
fill dem mind with lies!

and always

take dem by surprise!

food 4 thought!

separate unequal

20 sweet innocent babies are dead!

wasn't anything they did or said
wasn't so long ago they were born
and just like that they're gone!

and a nation cries and mourns
and a nation cries and mourns

all well and good, understood,

but…

who cries for the children of color
who die in da hood?

who cries for the children of color
who die in da hood?
how many…

and where are the politicians, media, celebs,
when one of our babies in da hood is shot dead?
when one of our babies in da hood is shot dead?

not a word is heard
or a politician calling the press
to a conference
expressing distress
about not 20 but many,
many, many, many, many,
hundreds, thousands of our innocent black & brown

precious best no longer around
'cause their little bodies have been laid
to rest in da ground!

their little bodies have been laid
to rest in da ground!

why the media and notables so vocal about 20
and not a word is said about the many,
many, many, many?

the silence cries out loud…

there seems to be a double standard around!
there seems to be a double standard around!

food 4 thought!

self

deprecating array of behavior on display
see the results in the world day to day
not intended to be that way
on part of said participants
nonetheless they are the recipients,
edged on by facilitators' corruption,
greed the common denominator

always the greed of evil men
who believe it will benefit them
then put blame on the victims
who suffer after they trick dem

so sad can almost laugh
like you broke my legs and blamed me
because i can't run a hundred yard dash
and taunt me like "what's wrong with you?"

the traits of evil reiterate,
reinforce, regenerate
the quality of life of people
slowly disintegrate
intensely intensifies in fahrenheit
and centigrade

such is the result of preyed upon folk,
hemmed up, yoked,
the notice said,

condition rarely addressed,
spoke to insure status quo,
grows, flourishes, remains the same in vogue
while mankind suffers in silence
freedom will be denied us

speak up so their plots are foiled
don't squeaky wheels get the oil?

food 4 thought!

you

got nothing for me Ya Nas, oh man
you can't benefit one when you need benefit too
you can't remind me what's best to do
what, why i really shouldn't do
whom i should listen to
the only source that's proven true
the only resource that can help you
the one and only that made you
gave you life,
equipped with faculties,
first and foremost the ability to breathe,
minds to think, discern, learn, speak
all the things one needs to succeed
knowledge to pick harvest, not weeds
nourishment to feed the spiritual, mental

physical needs can be acquired
only from the one and only
that created all things
from nothing came into being
simply by saying "be"
and it was, and it is

man, yo man, you can't do a thing for me!
you who can't even do for you
how you gonna help me?

look what you already did to those
who now or once lived
you made from fluid, despised

stand up an open adversary,
questioning everything
the very purpose of living
don't know a thing
that hasn't been revealed
and you took credit
for all you could steal
when without mercy
your existence wouldn't be real
your sustenance would not consist of a single meal
and yet you live by what you feel
even though in your little minds
your perceptions, understanding aren't real

man, you can't do a dam' thing for me!

except what you already showed me
that what gave and gives me misery
to this very day

food 4 thought!

living

to exist status quo perpetually
resisting what's right especially
conceptually, morally
to avoid controversy
is not living but a travesty
abdicating responsibility to
support, establish stability
based on what's fundamentally
essential in the promotion of justice
without bias, corruption in reality

not merely an assumption
that would be implemented ideally
but is far from fruition really
here now is the hour
power concedes only to power
freedom ain't free
nobody will just give it to you or me
not business as usual, hidden behind
empty patriotic slogans without substance
designed to render euphoric splendor
while evil soars, puss filled ooze festers,
infecting all of us

if justice excludes just a few,
the level playing fields are for them
not you!

food 4 thought!

masterminds

got lots to say
especially the vast wisdom they display
the ideas they share everyday
just look at the world today
results of lots of brilliant minds
helped make it this way

why the poverty in places
where there's so much for everybody
but enjoyed by a only a few

just thank the brilliant minds

more homeless in places
where others have more than
they even know what to do

remember the brilliant minds

oppression of the peoples' rights
mass murders
if they even think to fight
to advance their rights further

brilliant isn't it?

just look at this wonderful array of leadership,
leading the way by example
why aren't their lavish lives a sample?
why isn't their caring benevolence ample?

such brilliance to behold
that exploit the masses, young and old

why more brilliance
you couldn't imagine if you try
put these brilliant minds in birds
they would never fly

food 4 thought!

floodgates

opened to accommodate hate
lots available to date
plots possibly traced
but oh soooooo late

they already unlocked the floodgate
came through with 9mm
Glock, loaded, cocked,
ready to rock
man knows how to tear down
not build up

life…

hoods coming in the night
could be you or me tonight
life's full of fright
shredded peace in pieces
dreaded beast released
headed off to feast
taking heads off at least
this head's up to speak
about wassup
evil has come up
from places dug up beneath
now at ground level as we speak
ready to wreak, reek, unleash
mayhem on the weak

pray dem defeat!

put your hands up for real!

seeking deliverance from evil…

food 4 thought!

he vies

for the dünya*
lives lies for the dünya
compromises for the dünya
tries on disguise for the dünya
relies on a prize in the dünya
replies to the cries of the dünya
"come now and try me on for size"
says the dünya,
"you'll be pleasantly suprised",
said the dünya
"you're created to strive",
says the dünya,
"indulge and you'll soon fly like birds,
listen to my whispers,
pay attention to my words,
come now and sell your soul!
from now on you'll be on a roll
feed your flesh "f[..]k your soul"

this ancient test has been given
since mankind has been livin'
even fooled Adam (aws) wa Howa (aws)
mankind's mother and father
created from the Qadr, decree
from the Creator saying "Be"

lived in paradise
so nice, no words could suffice
but eat of the forbidden fruit
from the forbidden tree,
enticed by the lies of Shaitan's invite

even though they were warned
clear 'n loud,
"fear and obey your Lord's instruction!
he, Shaitan is your enemy avowed,
listening to his lies will lead to your destruction"

such is the fate of those
who compromise their faith
to this very day
the test remains the same
so ignore the dünya
when it calls your name
it's promises are lies designed
to compromise lives
lure you, implore you,
take you by surprise
fake you out, take your prize:
your soul

and on and on it goes
as mankind spirals out of control

food 4 thought!

~ ~ ~

* Dünya: An Arabic word with its phonetic spelling in Turkish, meaning "world".

frontal lobotomy

the vegetative state
what's left of me
not the way Allah (SWT) created me

opened my mouth
and my brain was taken to be studied
in some state sponsored lab ladder

lab rats in a nation
where they use behavioral modification
if what you got to say resonates
with a significant population,
igniting thought, raising consciousness
make dem get up, stand up, speak up for their rights
speaking truth to power
seeking justice
must be intelligent, thought out
not just spewing words out the mouth
chanting empty slogans
then get arrested, beat'
only for the same ol', same ol' repeat
innocent children gunned down in the street

they always wanted you to smile
even while the bodies pile
keeping the people docile

Poetic Snacks for the Conscious Munchies

we'll just keep your brains awhile,
you'll be good to go,
as we maintain the status quo
reduced to data
like Hannibal Lector
serving your brains up on a platter…

food 4 thought!

i look

around town, city, village
the world around
sometimes it seems
there's no taqwa* to be found
by the sights, sounds
what people do, hitting ground,
running to sin
where's the taqwa within?

even your own blood indulging

nobody's left unscaved,
mankind became a slave of flesh
might be time to retrieve to cave 'til death

time's getting worse yet
future to be a true test
only maghfirah**, Rahman Raheem***
will see you through
never a thing attributed to me or you
because we're weak. repleated with sin
need forgiveness wa nasrul' Allah (SWT)****,
to get cleaned within taqwa becoming rare

less 'n' less insha'Allah***** i hear
"i'll do this, that, meet you over there"
like the next second is a given
look how mankind is living
where's the taqwa?
where's the godly fear?

it's bad,
sad,
beyond tears
seems even those you love don't care
talking family dear
"do i know em, who's that over there?"

as we travel forward,
toward mankind's disaster
getting closer to Qiyamah******
faster and faster, year after year!

food 4 thought!

～ ～ ～

.

*taqwa: "fear of Allah" in Arabic.
**maghfirah: "forgiveness from Allah" in Arabic.
***Rahman Raheem: "mercy" in Arabic.
****wa nasrul' Allah: "the help of Allah (SWT)" in Arabic.
*****insha'Allah: "if Allah (SWT) wills" in Arabic.
****** Quiyamah: "Last Day" or "Judgment Day" in Arabic.

hitting the

path
walked long before you were born
narrow-filled, complete with thistles, thorns
broken glass, body remains turned to ash
blood stains splashed on the narrow but straight path
all signs point:
the righteous were here,
carrying great weight to bear
kept eye on the prize, overcame fear
even though the prize often seemed far hardly near
they knew the promise of Allah (SWT) is true
worth the wait what's waiting for you

faithful slaves who were willing
and gave the world away
for a better place that never goes away
feared their Lord and the Judgment Day
to enjoy gardens beneath which rivers flow
with milk and honey, time doesn't go
nobody grows old
unlike the plight of the crooked path
that looks good, wide and smooth
says "come on, we got something for you to adore,
it will adore you, you'll keep wanting more,
it keeps wanting you"

Poetic Snacks for the Conscious Munchies

sounds profound, to good to be true
that's why this path is made
to look and sound to accommodate you
hem you in sin, hypnotize, misguide
the glitter takes you by surprise,
blinds spiritual eyes
on this path, seemingly a smooth ride,
is deception, the element of surprise
waiting to lay waste to misguide
mankind who hurried in haste
left the prize behind, lost the race
never to taste the heavenly wine,
silk pillows to recline, dine with those
who wisely took the path free of wrath

divine bliss is bestowed on those
who chose and pursued
this ultimate, eternal, merciful gift
and ultimately enjoy the last laugh
that comes with it

food 4 thought!

exploring

levels of development
ignoring Shaitan's hand
on the plan
or you can…

look before you leap,
seek refuge from evil,
thank in gratitude
for the spiritual meal,
feeling guidance for real,
seeking refuse from evil,
refusing offers
of the devil's deal

compromise is also real,
always on the prowl
Hizbul-Shaitan* is poised to steal
your good deeds,
using fair-seeming bait as feed,
cruising around town
to set down on your needs,
something you can use in the hope
it's an offer you can't refuse,
then bring you to your knees

you've just been used!

they take off, looking for victims,
always ready to pick 'em,
skilled, using illusions to rope them
into a state of confusion,
as if they doped them, hooked to an IV
of trickery and transfusion

only one antidote to stay aware
you must adhere
to what Allah (SWT) spoke,
wrote, revealed
to repel, revoke what the devil tries to steal

yo!
think before you act,
ask Allah (SWT) to take your back,
the only one you came from
and to whom you surely must go back

the unseen is real!

food 4 thought!

~ ~ ~

*Hizbul-Shaitan: "Devil's Army" in Arabic.

SO

particles of love
floated to earth
enhanced man's rebirth
gave mankind a chance,
hovering for an instant
from a distance,
observing the wreck
called mankind,
falling to the ground,
tossed around, ignored
ridiculed love rebuked,
evil resolute to invoke dispute

the result, absolute!

mercy, justice, human rights
marginalized

relationship between individuals, nations,
compromised

by hidden agenda, lies
turns out to be hatred in disguise

sun doesn't shine, birds don't fly
you ask why?

when sincerity, honesty, humility,
basic divine qualities are not to be found,
basically disappear
soon to be but a memory everywhere

results: mankind in despair,
damaged beyond repair

when love is to be found nowhere,
blackened are the skies
to no surprise
mankind dies!

food 4 thought!

Musafah*

*For My Beloved Brother Bilal, Ra***

you're moving through
not to linger life's journey
swift part of the greater trip

don't fall in love with it!
don't become enthralled with it!
it won't love you back
no matter how many years are stacked
what appears to appear to be
lengthy, friendly
disappears shortly,
leaving many empty, disappointed

ya (oh) Musafah, are you special,
blessed, anointed?

you're traveling through to pass the test
until the time appointed
your soul will leave with your last breath
snatched away by the angel of death,
continuing the journey to what awaits next,
all in the process called the test

Musafah, ya Musafah,
may your journey be blessed!
may the Malaika*** say your name
in the place of bliss,
give you salutation,
say assalaamu alaykum wa rahmintu
lahi wa barakatu****,
may the peace and blessings of Allah (SWT) be upon you!

ya Musafah,
go in peace back to Allah (SWT),
you have traveled far…
welcome home forever!

food 4 thought!

~ ~ ~

*Musafah: Islamic name.
**Ra: The tenth letter of the Arabic alphabet.
***malaika: "Angels" in Arabic.
**** "may peace be upon you and the mercy and blessings of Allah (swt)

they

gathered in the public square
frustration, anger, fear
was hanging in the air,
like a storm cloud, ready to go
question not if but when

nobody knows
that's usually how the story goes
conceptually how this life flows,
when finally the cloud bursts,
tyranny can bring out the best and the worst

often it's a society's curse
because dem not adhere to the divine verse,
instead followed their flesh first
sometimes people get what they deserve,
including tyrants that rule cruel
not serve

ahead awaits the people's fate
fruits of duties, abated,
can include people immersed in self-hatred
receive consequences not perceived
but nonetheless related
to forbidden deeds
such is the effect of planting bad seeds

so reflect on cause and effect
before you demand respect!
or better yet,
look at what your own hands bring!

the next time the storm clouds bring
wind and rain
no surprise!

likewise…

sin brings pain

respect
cause 'n' effect

food 4 thought!

do

you bring a knife to a gunfight?

now you know that ain't right!

do you use weights to fly a kite?
now you know that ain't right!

do you yell out how much, in your wallet
while walking the streets late at night?
now you know that ain't right!

do you lay down
in the middle of I-95
on the Delaware-Maryland line
and expect to rise up alive?
now you know that ain't right!

no more than bringing that knife to a gunfight

tell me is that wrong or right?
maybe i'm not thinking right
pull my coat if my mind's in a float
if i fell overboard
pull me back in the boat

sooo

if you think that logic is not that remote
what i previously spoke,
then why the f[…]k do you stare down
some dam' army with AR-15s,
Humvees, killer dogs, racist cops
who don't want you alive no mo',
and say, "can we just get along"

sing the "Kumbaya",
"we will overcome" song?

you look at that picture
and see nothing wrong?
give me some of what you're on!
maybe i need to float off the ground

you mean you can't understand
how funky that sounds?

yesterday, today, tomorrow
nothing new 'bout dat

every second, minute, hour after hour
power never did and never will
concede to a thing but power,
and if you think bringing a knife
to a gunfight ain't the right bet,
how do you think yelling
"NO JUSTICE NO PEACE"
in the face of the beast
gonna get you respect?

you agree or disagree, maybe
but remember
something doesn't work
and you do the same thing over 'n' over,
again expecting different results
is the definition of crazy!

food 4 thought!

light

emanates piercing darkness,
reflective of truth, overpowers falsehood
one little ray of nur*
disperses dark ignorance
goes away
can't stay
in the company of bright rays

truth comes and
beats the brains out of falsehood
just as evil is trumped by good
love overpowers hate

such is the power of the divine light
rays of truth shine bright,
pierce darkness of the night,
send ignorance to flight
forbid evil, enjoin right,
assigned to the righteous,
this noble plight

this is the purpose of life
created to worship, praise the Creator,
from where you came,
commissioned to glorify His name,
hear and obey, remind mankind
of the words of Allah (SWT)

say
put that into practice
everyday
not the lip-service way

words, a mirror of your deeds,
for you are to be a beacon,
lighting the way,
a lamp onto the feet,
rendering falsehood running away
in full defeat,
bearing witness to the sound of Shaitan
in retreat

food 4 thought!

~ ~ ~

nur: A noun meaning "light" in Arabic.

tell me

whisper in my ear
tell me what i wanna hear

complements get you everywhere
regardless, if the truth appears or disappears,
included or excluded

who cares?

because bu!!$#!+ rules
everywhere there's fools
and fools appear everywhere

substance, relevance,
even uncommon sense
appear lost in life's course,
gone away, seemingly undetected
unnoticed, no remorse reflected,
wisdom disrespected

not unlike casting pearls before swine,
unappreciative of the value at the time

seems like dumbing down goes down fine,
like sipping ol' fine wine
the MO of the time

fake is in and real died
as they tried on
phony body parts for size
amidst "Give me new tits and ass"

Poetic Snacks for the Conscious Munchies

the background chorus, set on blast
investing in $#!+ that doesn't last
common sense and sanity
now a thing of the past

food 4 thought!

to rely

on man, mankind's words,
deeds, consistency, dependability,
honesty, sensitivity…

honesty borders on insanity

such is the caliber of humanity!

people you think you know,
even close blood family,
can and will flip instantly,
trip, no warning nor indication
blindsided, taken by surprise
can't wrap your brain around
the numbness is profound
how does no answer sound?

you don't know anybody
trust that, take that to the bank…

only the Creator knows
only the Maker knows
the makeup of man's mind

is it an evil spell cast upon?
vulnerable, naive, unsuspecting,
trusting souls, or something
strange that lurks within?
only Allah (SWT) knows!

but trust me
to rely on humankind,
most certainly deaf, dumb, and blind,
is like sticking your head in the sand
while exposing your bare behind

nobody but Allah (SWT) knows
how the human mind goes
regardless how many so called experts
claim to know…

that's why psychiatrists have high rates of suicide,
trying to understand what's inside
can totally blow minds…

food 4 thought!

the time

is now or may never come
time that isn't yours nor mine
isn't yours nor mine to waste
tossed away in haste
for some trivial pursuit to participate
by the time you relate
may be too late

such is time in relation to fate
such is time, yours and mine
in relation to a pre-arranged date

sense of urgency on display,
knowing any day can be your last day
the first day
your present life's snatched away
can be today or certainly
will be one of these days

walk the earth everyday
as though today is the last day
grateful, humble, thankful for each and everyday

then your last day can be your best,
leading to what awaits forever,
the supreme reward from your Lord
for those who used the time best
and ultimately passed the test

food 4 thought!

real lights

illuminate, accentuate the truth

fake lights glitter, disguised as light,
are not real, designed to steal real light,
don't heal like real light,
are designed to deceive,
make you believe
glitter is light,
wrong is right
night is day,
day is night

not ever like…

real lights
that excite, enlighten, ignite right,
always winning the good fight,
vanquishing darkness
sending Shaitan away in flight

if you're really for right…

you'll always know the difference
between the real and the fake light

food 4 thought!

lifting

me up...

burdens stop
spiritual elevator going up

peace washes over me,
warmth of summer covers wounds sustained
like a sedative, relieving pain,
brings new beginnings back again

at least the hope that it can
release the spirit forces from deep inside
the fitrah within
often sleeps, comes alive, then vibes,
malaise subsides,
miraculous events, heaven sent,
fill you with gratitude
will you more altitude
to rise from slumber
welcome summer!
to be in that number that you hear
plays deep within
when the saints come marching in

oh what a feeling to be alive!

comes back to thrive again,
reviving the will
something money, materialism never will!

food 4 thought!

pour

milk 'n' honey into my cup!

divine nectar,
never get enough pleasure
from *Ar-Rahmin's endless,
inexhaustible treasures,
tapping the storehouse

earth's richness still bountiful,
though diminished from men's abuse,
doomed to get worse due to
exploitive, disrespectful, greedy use

nonetheless much is still left
in the Creator's treasure chest
and the rotation of creation goes on,
bringing with it renewal

the jewels of seasons change,
earth dies in winter,
then springs back to life again

look at the transformation!

clear signs, invoking validation
of divine revelation,
sent down before
to all tribes and nations,
reminding mankind
the power of the divine,
to bring hope to the hearts,
enlightenment to minds

behold the glow of a summer morning
we have all come to know
but do we really, though,
even stop to reflect the gifts bestowed,
through unmatched mercy,
never owed, always undeserved?

all this and yet you ask,
"and to whom and what do we owe
and to whom and what do we serve?"

food 4 thought!

～～～

Ar-Rahmin: "The Merciful" in Arabic.

returning

the cold of winter, harsh, taxing
fades into the background
back in the cycle
taking it's place
keeping pace

now comes respite

earth blooms back to life
behold the Creator's might
giver 'n' taker of life,
the architect, designer, the planner,
the engineer, the executer,
doesn't need any help
does it all by Himself

He says "Be" and it is,

wants winter, "Be" winter,
wants spring, "Be" spring,
wants summer, "Be" summer,
wants fall, "Be" fall

that simple, that's all!

and we all enjoy

do we ponder, wonder in awe,
or just simply enjoy and ignore
how we're here every minute, hour
day, month, and year?
through the mercy and the power
of He who put us here
and what's more…
He who did this does implore
be mindful of the purpose of it all!

from the one who willed it comes the command
"Fulfill it!"

food 4 thought!

a van

today's, tomorrow's coke can
maybe a button on an elevator
lives change, the common denominator,
not strange, arranged by the Creator

what's of this world doesn't stay
fades away
with or without sorrow
regardless
here today, gone tomorrow

and this is what you invest in?
even strive, lie,
live in high drive
to attain what stays behind
when we die,
competing in pain
all in vain
for things you may
or may not use

you lose without gain
things we choose to attain
bring what we can't sustain,
except perhaps a heart stain,
consequence of material possessed brains,
mired in a mute fluke

rather aspire than acquire
and live by the truth!

food 4 thought!

raised

to give praise on sundays
as the sunrays penetrate
through the stained glass
slashing the pews
as the parishioners pray in
full view
immersed in a curious world
exclusive of those who don't
look, talk and act like you!
a little bubble designed to
keep out trouble
but steeped in sin their lives
kith'n' kin, husbands, wives
insulated from folk deemed
hated, isolated away from
people of color, that other
from whom they remain
segregated!
taught bout dem 'n' those
folk ain't da same as our
folk!

and they grow up confined to
this mental yoke
closed mind, blind eyez
the whole wide world has been
shrunk down to a little corner
called white folks town, and
we don't want ya'll hanging round

and dem grow up!

and become your cops, judges,
doctors, nurses, lawyers, mayors,

prison jailers and jurors given the
job to sit judgement on those same
folk who their forefathers spoke
with all the distain they invoked,
all the hateful jokes, things they
say, day after day..,
poised to hand down a verdict
to put your brown 'n' black ass away
or just shot you down acting as judge 'n'
jury in yours 'n' my town without a worry
bout any sentence handed down!

and who da F%^# cares
that da system calls dem
a jury of your peers!
that without blinking will
put you away for years
or let a killer walk who walked
to stalk and kill a innocent 17 year
old boy at will, enjoying the laws that
gave him the privilege to do
it to mine 'n' yours!
like it's a game, playing with
toys that got souls, names
lives, sons, daughters, husbands

wives! but never does it connect
in their feeble mind speck
that the same folk of whom their
peeps spoke are human beings
who deserve the same things
beginning with..,

respect!!

Shareef Abdur - Rasheed

in Remembrance of
Sulaiman El Hadi
of
The Last Poets

MAKE IT TIGHT
in Remembrance of Sulaiman El Hadi

Musa said make it tight, letting cars in the ranks ain't right!
Sulaiman, time has come for your appointment
insha'Allah without disappointment
before the setting of the sun!
Sulaiman made it tight!
Sulaiman made it tight!
in his lifelong fight,
not to jade,
what is right!
not to trade,
what Allah gave,
but keep in sight,
the garden of delight!
he said blessed are those
who struggle, who say if Allah will
and impose no ill!
don't take the pill,
thou shall not kill!
Sulaiman said the oppressor's injustice ain't right!
in defiance
always dropping science!
Signs
of the time in rhyme!
stimulating insight,
Sulaiman kept it tight!
Forbidding Wrong,
in a song!

not the first nor the last poet enjoining what is right!
Sulaiman, time has come
your appointment!
insha' Allah without disappointment,
before the setting of the sun!
our brother faithful slave,
may Allah bless,
and forgive your transgress!
put bliss in your grave,
with the righteous you be raised!
Alhamdulil'lah you inspire me!
for Allah i love you and will miss you ahkee!
let's keep it tight!!

Shareef Abdur-Rasheed
Oct. 1995

~ ~ ~

This poem was written in honor of a dear friend, Sulaiman El Hadi, whose life had a meaningful impact on myself, my family and all whom were blessed to be touched by his insightful consciousness.

Sulaiman El Hadi was one of the founding members of the renowned Social Activist Poetic group, The Last Poets.

The body must absorb food to benefit from its nutrition.

Knowledge needs wisdom to benefit from its implementation.

~ Shareef Abdur - Rasheed

epilogue

Shareef Abdur - Rasheed
Poetic Snacks for the Conscious Munchies

About the Author

Shareef Abdur-Rasheed, AKA, Zakir Flo was born and raised in Brooklyn, New York. His education includes Brooklyn College, Suffolk County Community College and Makkah, Saudi Arabia. He is a Veteran of the Viet Nam era, where in 1969 he reverted to his now reverently embraced Islamic Faith. He is very active in the Islamic community and beyond with his teachings, activism and his humanity.

The author has led quite a storied life and has been exposed to, has broken bread and communed with many other artists, musicians, activists and social luminaries such as the Reverend Al Sharton, Sulaiman El Hadi and Jalal Mansor Nurradin from the original "Last Poets" and numerous others. He himself is an avid percussionist and has a great passion for the Congas and Timbales. He is a great lover of the Afro Cubano, Latin Jazz and Salsa. Throughout his childhood, his father had exposed him to many of the Jazz greats who have been through New York. The list is far too extensive to mention.

Shareef's spiritual expression comes through the persona of "Zakir Flo". Zakir is Arabic for "to remind". Never silent, Shareef Abdur-Rasheed is always dropping science, love, consciousness and signs of the time in rhyme.

Shareef is the patriarch of the Abdur-Rasheed family with nine children (six sons and three daughters) and forty-three grandchildren (twenty-six boys and seventeen girls) and one great granddaughter.

~ ~ ~

For more information about
Shareef Abdur-Rasheed,
visit his personal FaceBook page at:

http://www.facebook.com/shareef.abdurrasheed

What People Are Saying

No college or university teaches wisdom 101.

~ Shareef Abdur - Rasheed

what people are Saying

from my Son ... Shakeel Abdur-Rasheed

I just want to express my gratitude to a man named Shareef Abdur-Rasheed, who taught me the most valuable things in life that are the keys to my success. Who dedicated his life to instilling in me, my siblings and others the recognition of the Almighty Creator and our purpose of life to be righteous human beings first and foremost. Also his sacrifice in supporting me & the family with a livelihood that provided comfort and a foundation of moral upbringing, peace and safety. He has always been a friend, well-wisher for my success and happiness and most of all, a great example of a father.

I have known the intelligent and creative personality of Shareef Abdur-Rasheed, who always used his gift of eloquence or crafty and catchy poetry to express knowledge and wisdom to promote truth, justice and peace. Relevant to current matters dealing with humanity, Shareef has always been a dynamic motivational guide to the problems humanity faces in today's world, sharing his deep understanding and the purpose of life towards all solutions and true success.

Shakeel Abdul-Rasheed
Author of Dark Scam

what people are Saying

Kimberly Burnham, Ph.D.

Poetic Snacks for the Conscious Munchies by Shareef Abdur-Rasheed is a wonderful collection of *blowing riffs*. I have followed his work as part of the *Year of the Poet's* Poetry Posse and Inner Child Press for several years. Some of my favorite lines bring vivid images told in unique ways. "Liberates one / from what haste / makes waste made from mistakes" or "what's new / and becomes old before the day unfolds? / is it real what we hold or is it / void of substance like foam?" or "change hovers above / as we engage in love of ease, / of self-indulgence / that which creatures of comfort seek / as we speak."

Shareef sees the ugliness and blood in this world but he also sees the grace and peace. His words lead us to a better world inhabited by our better selves. One of the motifs running through Poetic Snacks for the Conscious Munchies is an urgency to see reality and then change, grow, and reach for something greater. "Here today gone tomorrow / used up all the time / you and i could borrow."

Fahredin Shehu, Ph.D.

Deciphering the Silent

Praise be to "The One", The Omnipotent

It is the creative impulse that never leaves one to rest without giving birth to a Beauty, disregard of time and age.

It is "RAHM" out of whom "The Rahman" a Qur'an-ic concept for Mercy derives. And "Rahm", means The Womb. In the case of Rasheed the Womb of Creativity gave birth to a discourse as one of many manifestations of Poetry, which may be largely abused just because of its material element, which is "the Word". I said "discourse" that is created within us, the reader's minds with photographic sense of perception of things. Given that the text itself visualized in such a photographic and mechanical perception, may be pictured as religious and this very fact creates delusion as most of our senses do. Indeed this is rather a manifestation of human transformation,

what people are Saying

experience, Craft and Art; a reflection of spiritual Metanoia, i.e. Maturity in the form of Poetry full of rhythm, musicality and potency through what he did, a real deciphering of the Silent, his silent word, giving also a sonorous dimension of his Word.

I don't often write the prefaces and reviews since most of the works offered to me nowadays, does not fulfill my gluttony for perfection of Beauty. I have an artistic and spiritual thirst that goes unfulfilled. First and foremost do not be disoriented as a reader of this very offering, for it may consequently appear to create a refusal of readership.

The work of Rasheed, and my words here are the argument, the delight for the Soul, and its conceptual outburst.

One man may be remembered in the History of Literature who wrote only one book for his lifetime, *The Book of Mirdad*, that man is Mikahil Naimy.

I hope Rasheed shall not extinguish his poetic zeal and inner fire of creation but offer more in other circumstances.

Thank you very much indeed Shareef Abdur-Rasheed for giving me an opportunity to sup the Nectar of your Word.

Indeed the Omnipotent is patient…

Fahredin Shehu

January the 5th, 2016
Prishtina
Kosovo

…Neve na mungon vokabulari tokësor për çështje qiellore.
…We lack terrestrial vocabulary for the celestial quest

http://www.fahredin-sh.blogspot.com/

what people are Saying

Janet Perkins Caldwell

Shareef Abdur-Rasheed, aka Zakir Flo is a man on a mission. This mission is to bring humanity together. To be more accepting of others. He not only touches on political, social and in general messages to humanity, he shouts them in a loving way to get our attention, to allow us to crawl out of our box of conformity. He allows us to see perhaps a different viewpoint that is penned here which helps us to reach our own mission in life.

His works contain facts to back his up message as he shares his personal perceptions and philosophies. I met Brother Shareef a few years ago and it has been my pleasure to read his works and to become his friend. His words are not just a testament to the man but a living wealth of knowledge and wisdom. I have nothing but love and respect for my Brother. His words will move you, cause you, to see more than yourself and to think for yourself.

I urge you to get a copy of *Poetic Snacks for the Conscious Munchies* and buy one for a friend. Please do share his links found in this book. Many blessings. Enjoy!

Peace and Love,

Janet P. Caldwell

COO- Inner Child
Author
www.janetcaldwell.com/

what people are Saying

Hamza Elhadi

It is not just rhetoric. It is not just words that rhyme. The entire body of each poem is in itself a Class, a Lesson, a Journey. Once you begin, you CAN NOT stop reading; you CAN NOT stop Exploring; You WILL NOT stop experiencing !

hamza elhadi

Gail Weston Shazor

I am intimately familiar with this man, Shareef Abdur Rasheed, his ink and his spirit. I have long admired him and i look forward to his monthly contributions as a member of *The Poetry Posse* to *The Year of the Poet* anthological series. It is a treat when i stumble across his offered verse on social media.

He humbly calls this a snack, but anyone familiar will understand that we have been invited to a feast. This is not a dinner, repast or a banquet, indeed nothing as refined as that. This is truly an *eat and lick your fingers* offering. Throughout this feast we are given bites of the exotic as Shareef plies our palates with Arabic and Kuranic mixed with a spoonful of every "coloredmanness". He ends every helping with a spoon of "food for thought".

.

We were all admonished while growing up that we didn't know whether we liked something that we did not try.

what people are Saying

Try this! Shareef Abdur-Rasheed has piled nourishment upon the table and invited us in . . . enjoy.

Gail Weston Shazor
Author, Poet & Friend

William S. Peters, Sr.

It is with a great amount of reverence, in truth, laced with an endearing bias that i offer these words about my Brother Shareef Abdur-Rasheed. He truly is my brother, the older brother i never could have for i too am an eldest child. A week does not go by that we are not on the telephone discussing such topics as our Spirituality, our Consciousness, or the Social Ills that affect this world of ours and that of our children to come. He is truly a mentor to the spirit of this man i call "me".

As you read through his verse, aka *Poetic Snacks*; look at the pictures he so graciously shared; read the endorsements of others, you too will get the feeling that Brother Shareef is truly a humble man who is concerned about our state of being, who loves his Creator, his Family and us all. He takes the time and makes the effort to speak into the darkness bringing light about a variety of issues that affect each of us . . . directly and indirectly.

what people are Saying

What can i say, i feel truly blessed to have been put on a path in my life to have encountered such a noble, humble and loving soul. This is reflected in his work.

Bless Up

Bill
Inner Child, CEO

Patriotism is the opium of the masses.

~ unknown

The Gallery

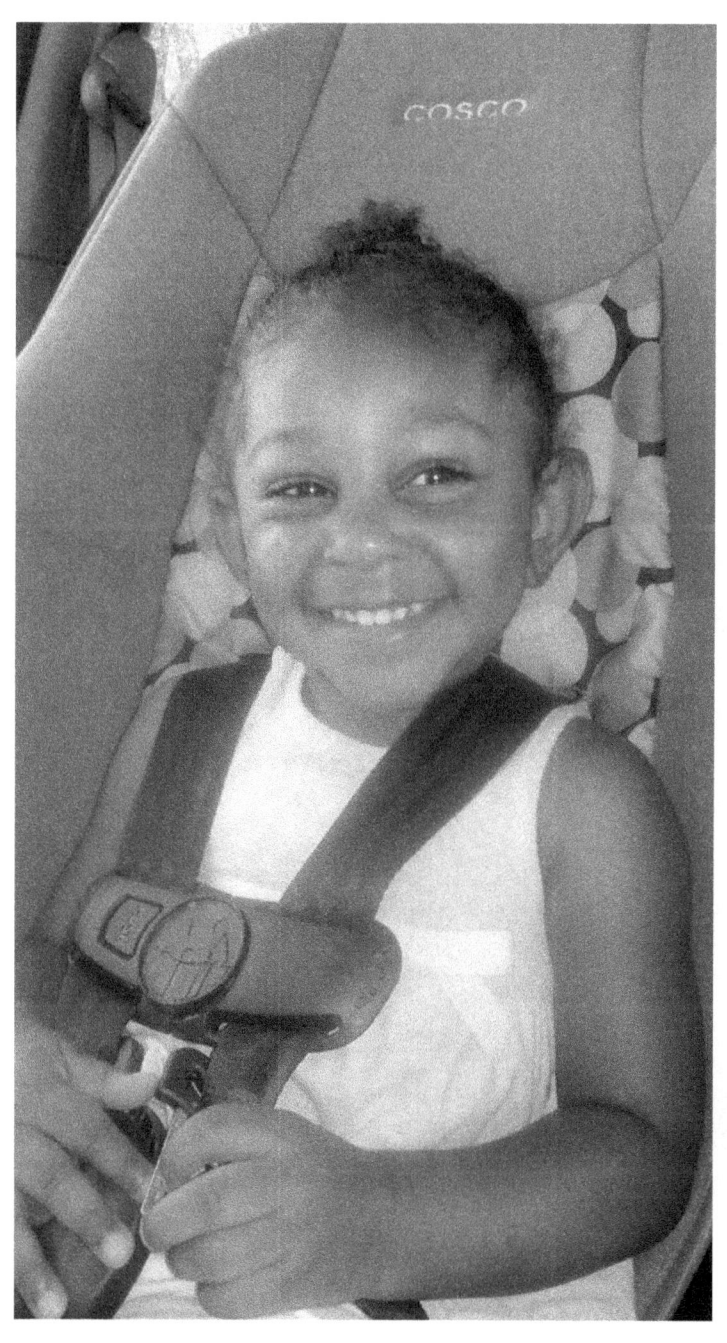

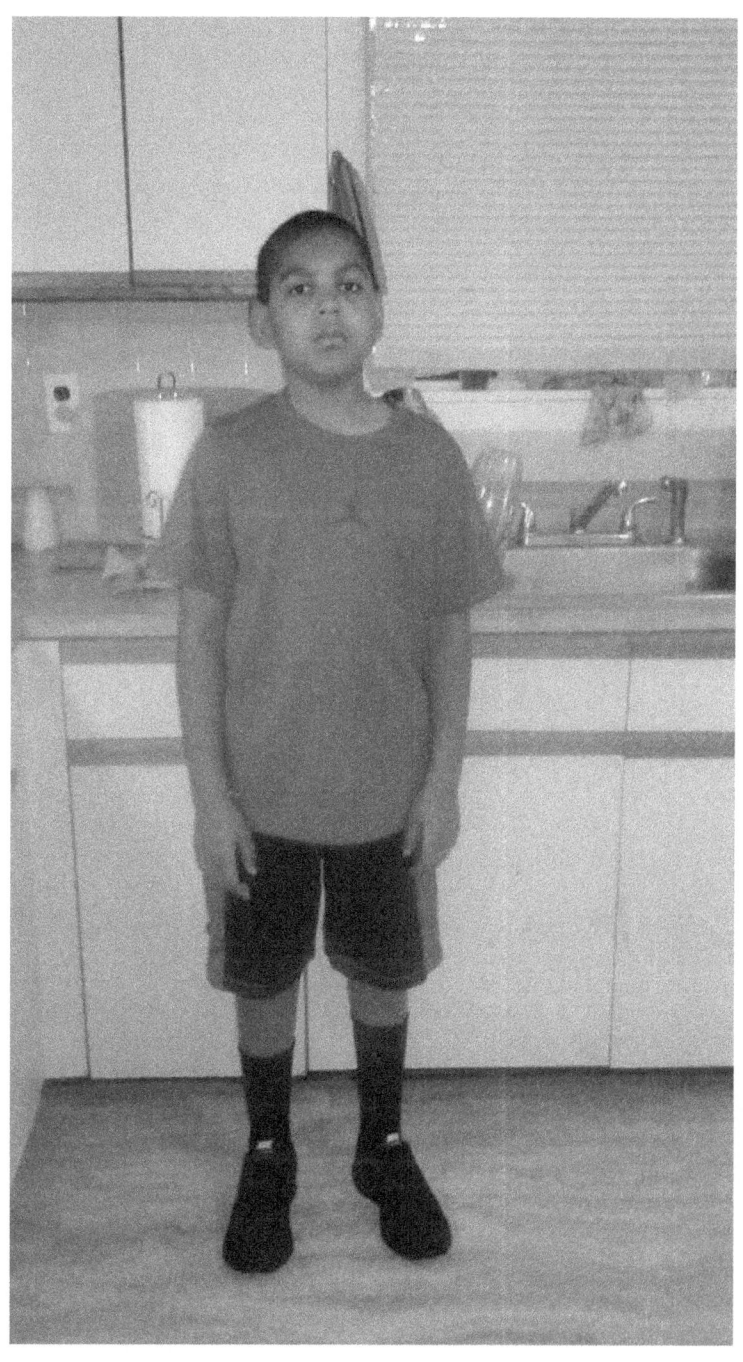

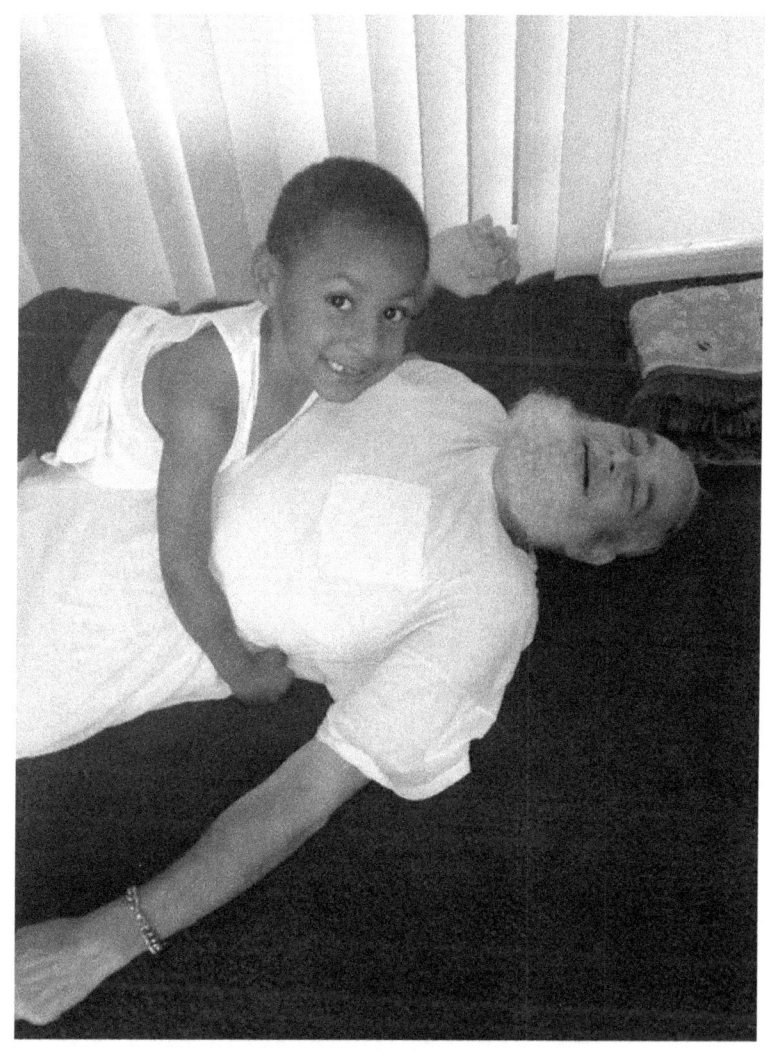

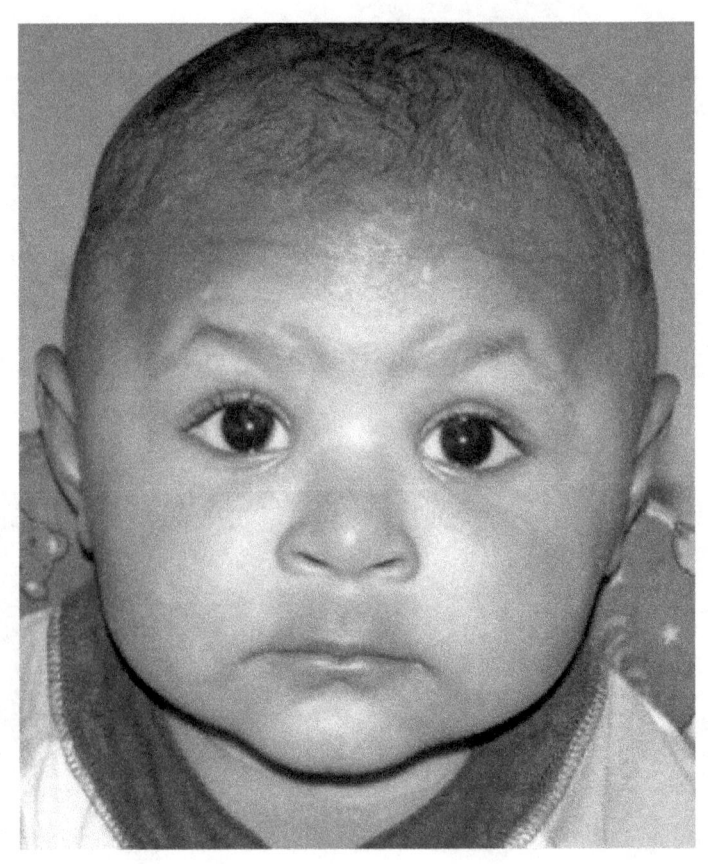

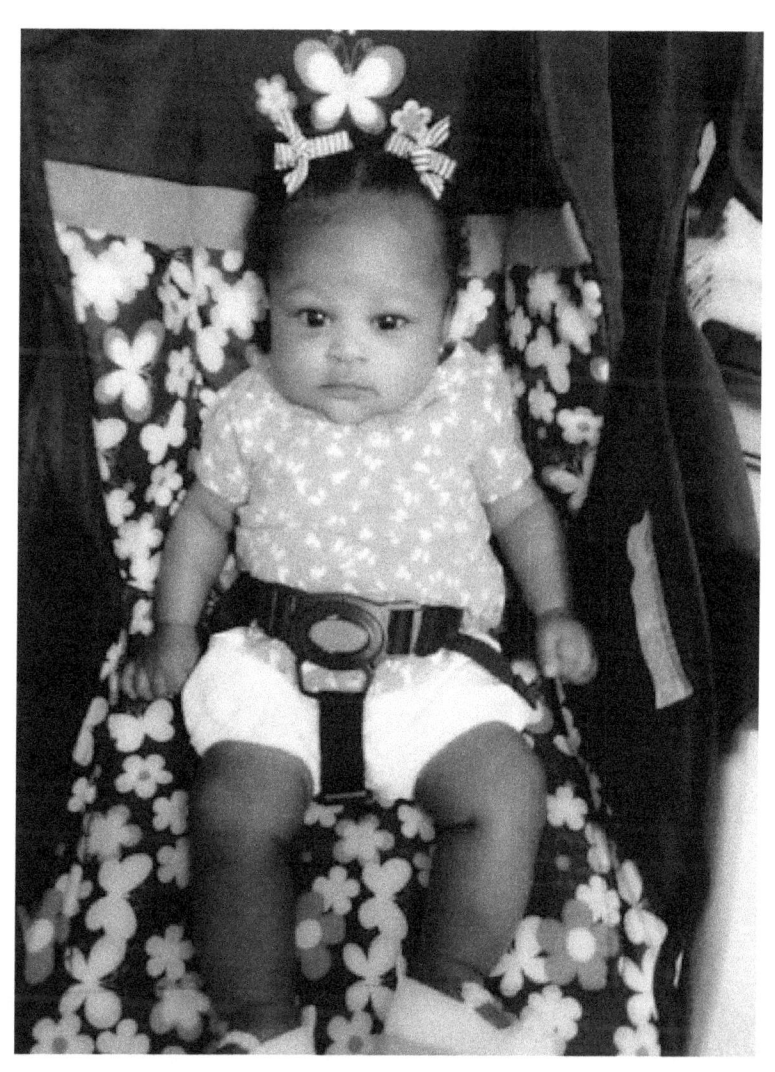

Inner Child Press

Inner Child Press is a publishing company founded and operated by writers. Our personal publishing experiences provide us an intimate understanding of the sometimes daunting challenges writers, new and seasoned may face in the business of publishing and marketing their creative "Written Work".

For more information

Inner Child Press

www.innerchildpress.com

intouch@innerchildpress.com

www.ingramcontent.com/pod-product-compliance
Lightning Source LLC
Chambersburg PA
CBHW061307110426
42742CB00012BA/2094